THE ULTIMATE GUIDE

THE GETTYSBURG ADDRESS

David Hirsch and Dan Van Haften

SB

Savas Beatie

California

First edition, first printing

ISBN-13: 978-1-61121-333-1

eISBN: 978-1-94066-967-0 (Savas Publishing Company)

Cataloging-in-Publication Data is available from the Library of Congress.

SB

Published by
Savas Beatie LLC
989 Governor Drive, Suite 102
El Dorado Hills, California 95762
Phone: 916-941-6896

Email: sales@savasbeatie.com
Web: www.savasbeatie.com

Savas Beatie titles are available at special discounts for bulk purchases in the United States by corporations, institutions, and other organizations. For more details, please contact Special Sales, P.O. Box 4527, El Dorado Hills, CA 95762, or you may email us at sales@savasbeatie.com, or visit out website at www.savasbeatie.com for additional information.

"In my position it is somewhat important that I should not say any foolish things."

Abraham Lincoln, November 18, 1863, one day before the Gettysburg Address.

Abraham Lincoln

Contents

Contents (continued)

The Speech

In his January 7, 1864, Annual Message, Pennsylvania Governor Andrew Curtin reported:

> After the battle of Gettysburg, in which loyal volunteers from eighteen States, including Pennsylvania, were engaged, it appeared to me proper that all those States should unite in establishing a Cemetery, on the spot in which their soldiers who had fallen in that conflict, should be honorably interred. I accordingly appointed DAVID WILLS, Esq., of Gettysburg, my agent, and through him, a site was purchased at a cost of $2,475.87, and the conveyances made to the Commonwealth. On communicating with the authorities of the other States, they all readily agreed to become parties to the arrangement, and on the 19th day of November last, the Cemetery was dedicated, with appropriate ceremonies, in the presence of the President of the United States, the Governors of the States concerned, and other high officers, State and National.[1]

On November 2, 1863, David Wills wrote President Lincoln: "It is the desire that, after the Oration [by featured speaker Edward Everett], You, as Chief Executive of the Nation, formally set apart these grounds to their Sacred use by a few appropriate remarks."[2]

At the November 19, 1863, ceremony, President Lincoln seated himself between Secretary of State William Seward and Edward Everett. Everett spoke for two hours. President Lincoln's 272 word speech was less than three minutes. On November 20, 1863, *The New York Times* reported:

> The military were formed in line extending around the stand, the area between the stand and military being occupied by civilians, comprising about 15,000 people and including men, women and children. The attendance of ladies was quite large. The military escort comprised one squadron of cavalry, two batteries of artillery and a regiment of infantry, which constitutes the regular funeral escort of honor for the highest officer in the service.
>
> After the performance of a funeral dirge, by BIRGFIELD, by the band, an eloquent prayer was delivered by Rev. Mr. STOCKTON...Mr. EVERETT then commenced the delivery of his oration, which was listened to with marked attention throughout...Although a heavy fog clouded the heavens in the morning during the procession, the sun broke out in all its brilliancy during the Rev. Mr. STOCKTON's prayer and shone upon the magnificent spectacle.

Reverend Stockton's prayer was over three times the length of the Gettysburg Address.

On November 20, 1863, Edward Everett wrote Abraham Lincoln, "I should be glad, if I could flatter myself that I came as near to the central idea of the occasion, in two hours, as you did in two minutes."[3]

This is how Lincoln biographer Michael Burlingame set the scene:

> After a musical interlude, Lincoln slowly rose to speak, causing a stir of expectation. His "reception was quite cordial," noted Benjamin Perley Poore. The Washington *Chronicle* reported that when [Ward Hill] Lamon introduced Lincoln, the president was "vociferously cheered by the vast audience." As spectators on the outer fringes of the crowd pressed forward, those closer to the platform pushed back, causing a brief disturbance. A nurse in the audience recalled that she and the others "seemed packed like fishes in a barrel," so tightly jammed together that they nearly suffocated. When calm was restored, the president put on his glasses, drew a paper from his pocket, and read his brief remarks "in a very deliberate manner, with strong emphasis, and with a most business-like air." His voice was so clear and loud that it carried to the outer extremities of the crowd. John Hay recorded in his diary that Lincoln spoke "in a firm free way, with more grace than is his wont."[4]

Gettysburg Address, November 19, 1863

The Gettysburg Address, November 19, 1863

Four score and seven years ago our fathers brought forth on this continent, a new nation, conceived in Liberty, and dedicated to the proposition that all men are created equal.

Now we are engaged in a great civil war, testing whether that nation, or any nation so conceived and so dedicated, can long endure. We are met on a great battle-field of that war. We have come to dedicate a portion of that field, as a final resting place for those who here gave their lives that that nation might live. It is altogether fitting and proper that we should do this.

But, in a larger sense, we can not dedicate—we can not consecrate—we can not hallow—this ground. The brave men, living and dead, who struggled here, have consecrated it, far above our poor power to add or detract. The world will little note, nor long remember what we say here, but it can never forget what they did here. It is for us the living, rather, to be dedicated here to the unfinished work which they who fought here have thus far so nobly advanced. It is rather for us to be here dedicated to the great task remaining before us—that from these honored dead we take increased devotion to that cause for which they gave the last full measure of devotion—that we here highly resolve that these dead shall not have died in vain—that this nation, under God, shall have a new birth of freedom—and that government of the people, by the people, for the people, shall not perish from the earth.[5]

The Structure of Reason Colorized

The Gettysburg Address neatly fits into a six element pyramid. Colorized pyramids show relationships among the elements.

Brown is factual foundation.

Green is logical direction.

Red is argument.

Think of the six elements of a proposition as a scientific method for persuasive speech.

The Gettysburg Address is special. Examination of its elements reveals precisely how. Brown, green, and red, are conceptual guides that highlight the purpose of each element.

Color lights up the speech like an X-ray or MRI. Brown represents factual foundation. Brown associates with the Given, Exposition, and Construction.

Green indicates logical progression. Green associates with the Sought, Specification, and Conclusion.

Proof (argument) is red. Red is like fire. It requires special handling.

The Gettysburg Address rises to a higher level when you understand brown, green, and red generally, and the elements specifically. So does appreciation for Abraham Lincoln's leadership skill. You will not only realize the special skill of the President, and the special nature of the Address; you will understand how it was accomplished.

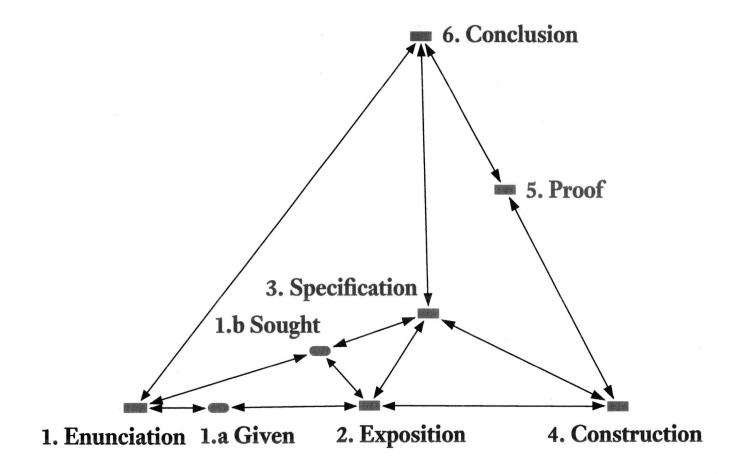

6. Conclusion

5. Proof

3. Specification

1.b Sought

1. Enunciation   1.a Given   2. Exposition   4. Construction

The Six Elements of a Proposition

1. Enunciation – "The enunciation states what is given and what is being sought from it."[6]

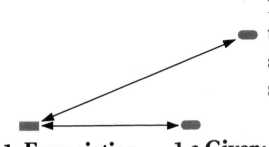

1.b Sought:
testing whether that nation, or any nation so conceived and so dedicated, can long endure.

1. Enunciation

1.a Given:
Four score and seven years ago our fathers brought forth on this continent, a new nation, conceived in Liberty, and dedicated to the proposition that all men are created equal. Now we are engaged in a great civil war,

The Enunciation answers the question: Why are we here?

The Given in the Gettysburg Address Enunciation begins: "Four score and seven years ago…"

A Given includes indisputable, basic facts.

The Enunciation's Sought is, "testing whether that nation, or any nation so conceived and so dedicated, can long endure."

A Sought is a relatively neutral statement of the general issue.

2. Exposition – "The exposition takes separately what is given and prepares it in advance for use in the investigation."[7]

1.b Sought:
testing whether that nation, or any nation so conceived and so dedicated, can long endure.

1. Enunciation

1.a Given:
Four score and seven years ago our fathers brought forth on this continent, a new nation, conceived in Liberty, and dedicated to the proposition that all men are created equal. Now we are engaged in a great civil war,

2. Exposition:
We are met on a great battle-field of that war.

The Exposition answers the question: What do we need to know relating to what is Given?

The Exposition factually sets the scene: "We are met on a great battle-field of that war."

The facts in an Exposition should be largely indisputable.

The rest of the speech examines what happened on that great battlefield, and reasons what needs to happen as a result.

3. Specification – "The specification takes separately the thing that is sought and makes clear precisely what it is."[8]

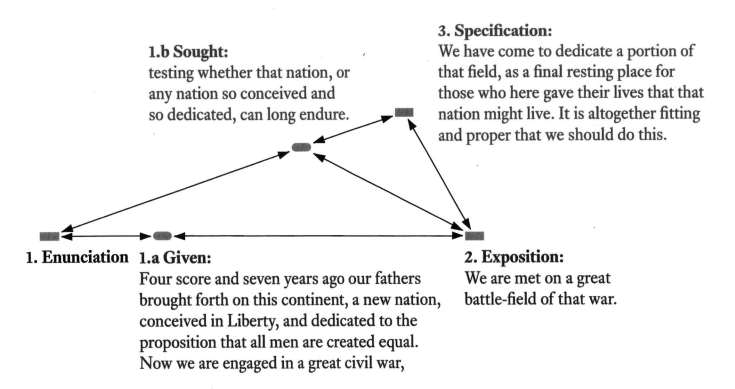

1.b Sought:
testing whether that nation, or any nation so conceived and so dedicated, can long endure.

3. Specification:
We have come to dedicate a portion of that field, as a final resting place for those who here gave their lives that that nation might live. It is altogether fitting and proper that we should do this.

1. Enunciation

1.a Given:
Four score and seven years ago our fathers brought forth on this continent, a new nation, conceived in Liberty, and dedicated to the proposition that all men are created equal. Now we are engaged in a great civil war,

2. Exposition:
We are met on a great battle-field of that war.

The Specification answers the question: What must be resolved to achieve what is Sought?

A Specification states the proposition more precisely than the Sought: "We have come to dedicate a portion of that field, as a final resting place for those who here gave their lives that that nation might live."

The Specification is the hypothesis to be proved. It is more specific than the Sought. While it does not need to be neutrally stated, neither does it need to be partisan. The key is it must be provable with facts and logic.

4. Construction – "The construction adds what is lacking in the given for finding what is sought."[9]

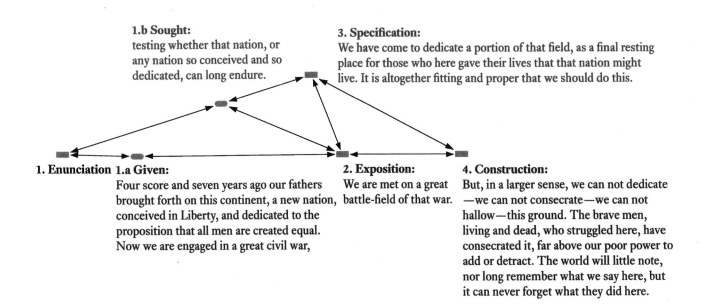

1.b Sought:
testing whether that nation, or any nation so conceived and so dedicated, can long endure.

3. Specification:
We have come to dedicate a portion of that field, as a final resting place for those who here gave their lives that that nation might live. It is altogether fitting and proper that we should do this.

1. Enunciation 1.a Given:
Four score and seven years ago our fathers brought forth on this continent, a new nation, conceived in Liberty, and dedicated to the proposition that all men are created equal. Now we are engaged in a great civil war,

2. Exposition:
We are met on a great battle-field of that war.

4. Construction:
But, in a larger sense, we can not dedicate —we can not consecrate—we can not hallow—this ground. The brave men, living and dead, who struggled here, have consecrated it, far above our poor power to add or detract. The world will little note, nor long remember what we say here, but it can never forget what they did here.

The Construction answers the question: How do the facts lead to what is Sought?

A largely fact-based Construction ends, "The world…can never forget what they did here." This leads to the Proof.

A Construction typically arrays facts to set up the Proof's argument. The Construction here is followed by a Proof that will argue what is left to do, so that "these dead shall not have died in vain".

5. Proof – "The proof draws the proposed inference by reasoning scientifically from the propositions that have been admitted."[10]

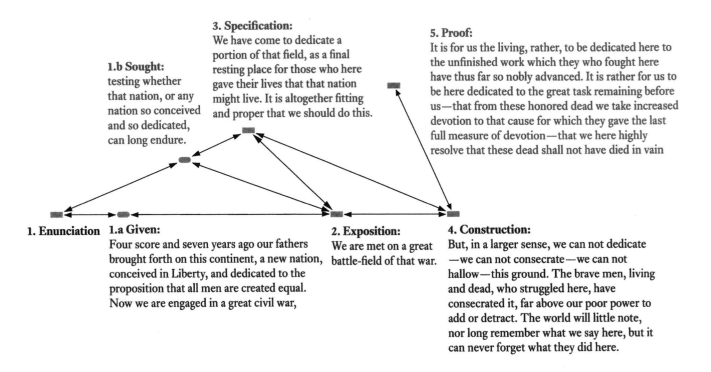

3. Specification:
We have come to dedicate a portion of that field, as a final resting place for those who here gave their lives that that nation might live. It is altogether fitting and proper that we should do this.

1.b Sought:
testing whether that nation, or any nation so conceived and so dedicated, can long endure.

5. Proof:
It is for us the living, rather, to be dedicated here to the unfinished work which they who fought here have thus far so nobly advanced. It is rather for us to be here dedicated to the great task remaining before us—that from these honored dead we take increased devotion to that cause for which they gave the last full measure of devotion—that we here highly resolve that these dead shall not have died in vain

1. Enunciation

1.a Given:
Four score and seven years ago our fathers brought forth on this continent, a new nation, conceived in Liberty, and dedicated to the proposition that all men are created equal. Now we are engaged in a great civil war,

2. Exposition:
We are met on a great battle-field of that war.

4. Construction:
But, in a larger sense, we can not dedicate —we can not consecrate—we can not hallow—this ground. The brave men, living and dead, who struggled here, have consecrated it, far above our poor power to add or detract. The world will little note, nor long remember what we say here, but it can never forget what they did here.

The Proof answers the question: How does the admitted truth confirm the proposed inference?

Argument naturally belongs in the Proof. Imperfectly timed argument loses credibility. Properly done, argument is credible and persuasive. Ideally, after the first four elements, the audience anticipates the Proof. If the nation will do what Lincoln argues it must, it will survive.

The Proof argues what those living must do for the nation itself to live:

1) …be dedicated here to the unfinished work…;
2) …be here dedicated to the great task remaining before us…;
3) …take increased devotion to that cause…; and
4) …highly resolve that these dead shall not have died in vain

Scientific reasoning draws the proposed inference. What started as a hypothesis is about to become a fact.

6. Conclusion – "The conclusion reverts to the enunciation, confirming what has been proved."[11]

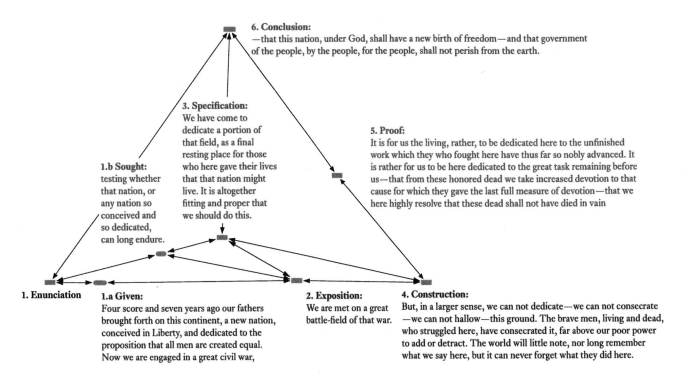

6. Conclusion:
—that this nation, under God, shall have a new birth of freedom—and that government of the people, by the people, for the people, shall not perish from the earth.

3. Specification:
We have come to dedicate a portion of that field, as a final resting place for those who here gave their lives that that nation might live. It is altogether fitting and proper that we should do this.

5. Proof:
It is for us the living, rather, to be dedicated here to the unfinished work which they who fought here have thus far so nobly advanced. It is rather for us to be here dedicated to the great task remaining before us—that from these honored dead we take increased devotion to that cause for which they gave the last full measure of devotion—that we here highly resolve that these dead shall not have died in vain

1.b Sought:
testing whether that nation, or any nation so conceived and so dedicated, can long endure.

1. Enunciation

1.a Given:
Four score and seven years ago our fathers brought forth on this continent, a new nation, conceived in Liberty, and dedicated to the proposition that all men are created equal. Now we are engaged in a great civil war,

2. Exposition:
We are met on a great battle-field of that war.

4. Construction:
But, in a larger sense, we can not dedicate—we can not consecrate—we can not hallow—this ground. The brave men, living and dead, who struggled here, have consecrated it, far above our poor power to add or detract. The world will little note, nor long remember what we say here, but it can never forget what they did here.

The Conclusion answers the question: What was proved?

The Conclusion reverts to the Sought. Lincoln's roadmap for the living is designed to ensure the nation survives: "—that this nation, under God, shall have a new birth of freedom—and that government of the people, by the people, for the people, shall not perish from the earth."

Logical Development

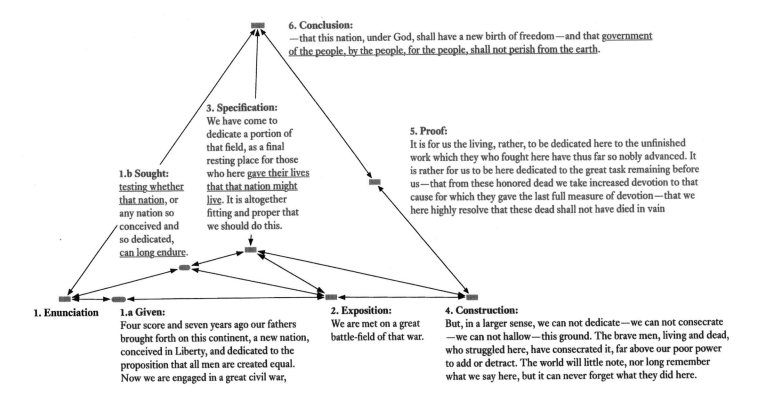

6. Conclusion:
—that this nation, under God, shall have a new birth of freedom—and that <u>government of the people, by the people, for the people, shall not perish from the earth.</u>

3. Specification:
We have come to dedicate a portion of that field, as a final resting place for those who here <u>gave their lives that that nation might live</u>. It is altogether fitting and proper that we should do this.

5. Proof:
It is for us the living, rather, to be dedicated here to the unfinished work which they who fought here have thus far so nobly advanced. It is rather for us to be here dedicated to the great task remaining before us—that from these honored dead we take increased devotion to that cause for which they gave the last full measure of devotion—that we here highly resolve that these dead shall not have died in vain

1.b Sought:
<u>testing whether that nation</u>, or any nation so conceived and so dedicated, <u>can long endure.</u>

1. Enunciation

1.a Given:
Four score and seven years ago our fathers brought forth on this continent, a new nation, conceived in Liberty, and dedicated to the proposition that all men are created equal. Now we are engaged in a great civil war,

2. Exposition:
We are met on a great battle-field of that war.

4. Construction:
But, in a larger sense, we can not dedicate—we can not consecrate—we can not hallow—this ground. The brave men, living and dead, who struggled here, have consecrated it, far above our poor power to add or detract. The world will little note, nor long remember what we say here, but it can never forget what they did here.

Note the underlined portions of the Sought, Specification, and Conclusion in the pyramid. Logical development (green) begins with a general statement of what is Sought: "testing whether that nation…can long endure." It progresses to a Specification that functions as a hypothesis: "…gave their lives that that nation might live…" It ends with a Conclusion that confirms what was proved: "…government of the people, by the people, for the people, shall not perish from the earth." This is the logical flow.

Logical development rests on fact (brown: Given, Exposition, and Construction). The Given states, "Four score and seven years ago our fathers brought forth on this continent, a new nation…" That statement is not disputable. The Given concludes, "…conceived in Liberty, and dedicated to the proposition that all men are created equal. Now we are engaged in a great civil war." The way President Lincoln states it, that too is indisputable.

The Exposition adds, "We are met on a great battle-field of that war." That is not disputable.

Facts asserted in the Construction are not controversial. In 1863, the speech's Construction was fairly indisputable. The Construction marshals facts that lead to the Proof.

The Proof is the second to last element. It contains perfectly timed argument with a foundation of largely indisputable fact (brown). Logical development (green) weaves around fact. Both funnel through the argument in the Proof, to reach a self-evident Conclusion.

Linear Demarcation
The Gettysburg Address
November 19, 1863

1. Enunciation: "States what is given and what is being sought from it."

[Given] Four score and seven years ago our fathers brought forth on this continent, a new nation, conceived in Liberty, and dedicated to the proposition that all men are created equal. Now we are engaged in a great civil war, **[Sought]** testing whether that nation, or any nation so conceived and so dedicated, can long endure.

2. Exposition: "Takes separately what is given and prepares it in advance for use in the investigation."

We are met on a great battle-field of that war.

3. Specification: "Takes separately the thing that is sought and makes clear precisely what it is."

We have come to dedicate a portion of that field, as a final resting place for those who here gave their lives that that nation might live. It is altogether fitting and proper that we should do this.

4. Construction: "Adds what is lacking in the given for finding what is sought."

But, in a larger sense, we can not dedicate—we can not consecrate—we can not hallow—this ground. The brave men, living and dead, who struggled here, have consecrated it, far above our poor power to add or detract. The world will little note, nor long remember what we say here, but it can never forget what they did here.

5. Proof: "Draws the proposed inference by reasoning scientifically from the propositions that have been admitted."

It is for us the living, rather, to be dedicated here to the unfinished work which they who fought here have thus far so nobly advanced. It is rather for us to be here dedicated to the great task remaining before us—that from these honored dead we take increased devotion to that cause for which they gave the last full measure of devotion—that we here highly resolve that these dead shall not have died in vain

6. Conclusion: "Reverts to the enunciation, confirming what has been proved."

—that this nation, under God, shall have a new birth of freedom—and that government of the people, by the people, for the people, shall not perish from the earth.

The Evidence

Abraham Lincoln had less than one year of formal education. Speaking in the third person in a short 1860 autobiography, presidential candidate Abraham Lincoln wrote:

> After he was twentythree, and had separated from his father, he studied English grammar, imperfectly of course, but so as to speak and write as well as he now does. He studied and nearly mastered the Six-books of Euclid, since he was a member of Congress.[12]

In 1849, Abraham Lincoln returned to Illinois after one two-year term in Congress. He resolved to become a better speaker. Lincoln studied the first six books of Euclid's *Elements of Geometry* to learn what it means to demonstrate. Euclid used the six elements of a proposition to prove theorems of plane geometry. The definitions of the six elements were preserved by Proclus, a fifth century philosopher who wrote commentary on Euclid's *Elements of Geometry*.[13]

Abraham Lincoln's writing from 1854 on is the best evidence of his structural writing technique.

The Gettysburg Address

Four score and seven years ago our fathers brought forth on this continent, a new nation, conceived in Liberty, and dedicated to the proposition that all men are created equal. Now we are engaged in a great civil war, testing whether that nation, or any nation so conceived and so dedicated, can long endure. We are met on a great battle-field of that war. We have come to dedicate a portion of that field, as a final resting place for those who here gave their lives that that nation might live. It is altogether fitting and proper that we should do this. But, in a larger sense, we can not dedicate—we can not consecrate—we can not hallow—this ground. The brave men, living and dead, who struggled here, have consecrated it, far above our poor power to add or detract. The world will little note, nor long remember what we say here, but it can never forget what they did here. It is for us the living, rather, to be dedicated here to the unfinished work which they who fought here have thus far so nobly advanced. It is rather for us to be here dedicated to the great task remaining before us—that from these honored dead we take increased devotion to that cause for which they gave the last full measure of devotion—that we here highly resolve that these dead shall not have died in vain—that this nation, under God, shall have a new birth of freedom—and that government of the people, by the people, for the people, shall not perish from the earth.

Other Evidence

While Abraham Lincoln's many writings that demarcate are the best evidence of his use of the six elements of a proposition, Lincoln left other evidence:[14] In the fourth Lincoln-Douglas Debate, September 18, 1858, Senator Stephen A. Douglas questioned a speech of U.S. Senator Lyman Trumbull by attacking Trumbull's integrity. Lincoln responded:

> Why, sir, there is not a word in Trumbull's speech that depends on Trumbull's veracity at all. He has only arrayed the evidence and told you what follows as a matter of reasoning. There is not a statement in the whole speech that depends on Trumbull's word. If you have ever studied geometry, you remember that by a course of reasoning Euclid proves that all the angles in a triangle are equal to two right angles. Euclid has shown you how to work it out. Now, if you undertake to disprove that proposition, and to show that it is erroneous, would you prove it to be false by calling Euclid a liar?[15]

When Lincoln spoke of arraying the evidence, he was referring to the fourth element, the Construction. When he said, "what follows as a matter of reasoning", he was referring to the fifth element, the Proof.

Senator Douglas advocated popular sovereignty; he wanted the western territories to individually choose whether to have slavery. Lincoln opposed popular sovereignty; Lincoln did not want to extend slavery in the territories. He challenged Douglas in an 1859 Columbus, Ohio, speech:

> Now, if Judge Douglas will demonstrate somehow that this is popular sovereignty—the right of one man to make a slave of another, without any right in that other, or any one else, to object—demonstrate it as Euclid demonstrated propositions—there is no objection.[16]

The May 12, 1865, *San Francisco Bulletin* attributed to Abraham Lincoln a conversation at an outdoor White House concert:

> I have through life been obliged to strip ideas of their ornaments, and make them facts before I conquered them. Euclid was my corner-stone, and the few flights I have taken in eloquence have never carried me out of sight of that hard basis. What began in a narrow necessity remains a habit, and I have but a dull sense of the beautiful; still, a few soft, heart-searching notes such as we hear now, will often remind me of want, convincing me that like other hard-workers, I may have gained in precision, concentration, or that hard power of arrangement we draw from mathematics, at the cost, may be, of the silent pleasure an eye educated to beauty can always drink in at a glance.[17]

Synergies

The payoff of internalizing the six elements for writing, speaking, reading, listening, and understanding, is handsome. Persuasive composition becomes easy. Critical analysis becomes automatic.

To understand any one element, there must be at least a rudimentary grasp of all six. While the six elements can be listed in linear order, they interact multidimensionally. Each element synergistically extends to the other five elements with simple elegance and textured complexity. The six element method of thinking and composition provides structure, location, and purpose for words. The six elements channel passion, and enhance expression.

The six elements of a proposition are ideally suited to well-prepared, careful drafting. Once internalized, the six elements can change the way you think and handle information. The six elements facilitate faster and better analysis.

A mind comfortable with the six elements can better deal with impromptu situations. The elements dynamically organize facts, perfectly weaving in logic. A fact-based Given (the first part of the Enunciation), a slightly more sophisticated fact-based Exposition, plus a largely fact-based Construction, form an anchor of truth. Logic develops on a foundation of fact. Everything is structured into the right place. Place is timing.

A six-element proposition begins with general, indisputable facts (the Given), followed by a neutral, high-level statement of what is Sought. The Given should recite the most basic, obvious, indisputable facts that will be built on. The Sought leads to additional needed facts (the Exposition) that lead to a precise Specification of what will be proved. The Gettysburg Address Sought, "testing whether that nation, or any nation so conceived and so dedicated, can long endure", is both neutral and general.

An Exposition factually builds without arguing. The Exposition recites additional facts that are necessary and obviously true.

The Specification asserts those buried on the battlefield "gave their lives that that nation might live."

Facts are arrayed in a Construction that lead to a Proof that scientifically proves precisely what was specified. The Construction can be innovative, simple, or complex. It can be short or long. It should be largely fact based. Even if complex, it must be understandable. It is the transition to argument (Proof). The Construction itself should not argue (at least not directly), or credibility is risked. A Construction sets up the Proof.

The Gettysburg Address Construction transitions, "But, in a larger sense, we can not dedicate—we can not consecrate—we can not hallow—this ground. The brave men, living and dead, who struggled here, have consecrated it, far above our poor power to add or detract. The world will little note, nor long remember what we say here, but it can never forget what they did here." This leads to the Proof that the living must (and presumably will) complete the unfinished work for the United States to survive. It argues what the living must do (complete the unfinished work) for the nation to survive "that these dead shall not have died in vain".

Facts are more important than logic. Without facts, there is nothing upon which logic can rest. The Gettysburg Address builds on a few general facts: the founding of the United States, the Civil War, a battlefield location, and the dedication of a cemetery. Facts provided the necessary foundation to logically demonstrate the nation's path to survival.

The Conclusion: "—that this nation under God, shall have a new birth of freedom—and that government of the people, by the people, for the people, shall not perish from the earth."

The six elements precisely control timing with perfect location for facts and logic. The result is iron logic anchored in firm factual foundation.

Timeline

Feb 12, 1809   Abraham Lincoln born.

Apr 8, 1826   Thomas Jefferson wrote Edward Everett regarding Jefferson's view on slavery.[18]

Jul 4, 1826   Thomas Jefferson died.

Aug 3, 1846   Abraham Lincoln elected as the only Illinois Whig representative in Congress.

Mar 4, 1849   Abraham Lincoln left Congress to return to law practice.

Mar 7, 1849   Abraham Lincoln presented his only oral argument before the U.S. Supreme Court.

1849-1854   Abraham Lincoln studied Euclid and the propositions of plane geometry.

Sep 18, 1858   Abraham Lincoln referenced Euclid in a challenge to Stephen A. Douglas in the fourth Lincoln-Douglas Debate.

Sep 16, 1859   Abraham Lincoln's Columbus, Ohio, challenge to Stephen A. Douglas on popular sovereignty included a reference to Euclid.

June 1860   In a short biographical statement, Presidential candidate Abraham Lincoln mentioned that Euclid contributed to his education.

Nov 2, 1863   David Wills wrote President Abraham Lincoln to request Lincoln deliver "a few appropriate remarks" at the Gettysburg National Cemetery dedication.

Nov 19, 1863   Edward Everett delivered a two-hour oration at the Gettysburg National Cemetery dedication.

Abraham Lincoln delivered the Gettysburg Address.

Nov 20, 1863   Edward Everett wrote Abraham Lincoln. Everett praised Lincoln's short speech.

Jan 7, 1864   Pennsylvania Governor Andrew Curtin reported on events related to the dedication of the Gettysburg National Cemetery.

Apr 14, 1865   President Abraham Lincoln was assassinated.

May 12, 1865   The *San Francisco Bulletin* printed a quotation attributed to Lincoln, that Euclid was his cornerstone.[19]

2010   *Abraham Lincoln and the Structure of Reason* revealed Abraham Lincoln's post-1853 use of the six elements of a proposition: Enunciation, Exposition, Specification, Construction, Proof, and Conclusion.

Presidents

President Thomas Jefferson used the six elements of a proposition. For example, in Chapter 13 of *Abraham Lincoln and the Structure of Reason,* the authors revealed Jefferson's use of the six elements of a proposition to compose the Declaration of Independence.[20]

Within weeks after receiving *Abraham Lincoln and the Structure of Reason,* President Barack Obama started to use the six elements of a proposition to structure his speeches. *Barack Obama, Abraham Lincoln, and the Structure of Reason* documents President Obama's adoption of the technique during the first half of 2011.[21] He used the six elements of a proposition to structure remarks delivered January 12, 2011, in Tucson, Arizona. The speech was at a memorial for six victims murdered at a constituent meeting with Gabrielle Giffords, a member of the U.S. House of Representatives.[22]

Gustav Niebuhr wrote in the *Huffington Post,* "Obama's 'Gettysburg Moment': For Us, the Living": "But the form Lincoln set at Gettysburg can be followed. . . The words spoken in 2011 follow the form laid down in 1863: out of tragedy, we seek meaning and national renewal."[23]

John McCain[24] and Peggy Noonan[25] also recognized something special in President Obama's Tucson speech.

Russell Allyn wrote an article titled, "Obama's Tucson Speech was his Gettyburg Address":

> In making his memorial speech in Tucson to honor those who were injured or killed last week, President Obama used many of the words and themes of the Gettysburg Address, along with those of Lincoln's other speech carved into the walls of his Memorial, his Second Inaugural Address.[26]

On February 28, 2013, Jon Favreau, President Obama's lead speechwriter, was interviewed by Stephen Colbert on *The Colbert Report*. In response to a question, Favreau said:

And, so when we sit down with a speech, we don't, we think less about the individual lines, or what's going to be quoted, or what the sound byte is, and what we make sure most of all is that we're telling a story from beginning to end, and that there's like a logical argument in the speech.[27]

Favreau's voice trailed off when he said, "and that there's like a logical argument in the speech." He seemed to complete the thought for the historical record, not for the present audience.

Former President Bill Clinton's September 4, 2012, speech at the 2012 Democratic National Convention in support of Barack Obama demarcates into the six elements of a proposition.[28] This is the only Bill Clinton speech we are aware of that demarcates.

Other Politicians and Public Figures

On January 1, 2012, presidential candidate and former House Speaker Newt Gingrich walked into Maccabbee's Deli in Des Moines, the day before the Iowa Caucus. He was three minutes early. The Speaker started shaking hands, maybe 10 seconds a person. David Hirsch was about the fourth person he shook hands with. David told Newt he wanted to give him a copy of a book about Lincoln that David co-authored. Speaker Gingrich looked at the cover, and asked, "Is this the book about Lincoln and geometry?" David said, "Yes." Newt said, "I have that book on my Kindle. It completely changed the way I give speeches."

Photograph by Dr. Alan Koslow

First lady Michelle Obama's September 4, 2012, speech at the Democratic National Convention demarcates into the six elements of a proposition.[29]

Endnotes

1. Regarding total state expenditures, Governor Curtin reported, "The expenses attending the establishment of this Cemetery, including the cost of the site and of removing the bodies of the slain, have thus far amounted to $5,209.38, and an appropriation will be required to pay these expenses, and to meet our portion of those attending its future maintenance." *Revised Report made to the Legislature of Pennsylvania, relative to the Soldiers' National Cemetery, at Gettysburg* (Harrisburg: PA: Singerly & Myers, State Printers, 1867), 3.

2. David Wills to Abraham Lincoln, November 2, 1863. Available at *Abraham Lincoln Papers at the Library of Congress*, Manuscript Division (Washington, D. C.: American Memory Project, [2000-02]), memory.loc.gov/ammem/alhtml/alser1_dates.html (accessed February 13, 2016).

3. Edward Everett, "Edward Everett to Abraham Lincoln, November 20, 1863," *The Collected Works of Abraham Lincoln*, ed. Roy P. Basler (New Brunswick, NJ: Rutgers University Press, 1953), 7:25 n1.

4. Michael Burlingame, *Abraham Lincoln: A Life, Vol. 2* (Baltimore, MD: The John Hopkins University Press, 2008), 573-574.

5. Abraham Lincoln, "FINAL TEXT: Address Delivered at the Dedication of the Cemetery at Gettysburg, November 19, 1863," *The Collected Works of Abraham Lincoln*, ed. Roy P. Basler (New Brunswick, NJ: Rutgers University Press, 1953), 7:22-23.

6. Proclus, *A Commentary on the First Book of Euclid's Elements, Translated with Introduction and Notes by Glenn R. Morrow* (Princeton, NJ: Princeton University Press, 1970), 159.

7. Proclus, *A Commentary on the First Book of Euclid's Elements, Translated with Introduction and Notes by Glenn R. Morrow* (Princeton, NJ: Princeton University Press, 1970), 159.

8. Proclus, *A Commentary on the First Book of Euclid's Elements, Translated with Introduction and Notes by Glenn R. Morrow* (Princeton, NJ: Princeton University Press, 1970), 159.

9. Proclus, *A Commentary on the First Book of Euclid's Elements, Translated with Introduction and Notes by Glenn R. Morrow* (Princeton, NJ: Princeton University Press, 1970), 159.

10. Proclus, *A Commentary on the First Book of Euclid's Elements, Translated with Introduction and Notes by Glenn R. Morrow* (Princeton, NJ: Princeton University Press, 1970), 159.

11. Proclus, *A Commentary on the First Book of Euclid's Elements, Translated with Introduction and Notes by Glenn R. Morrow* (Princeton, NJ: Princeton University Press, 1970), 159.

12. Abraham Lincoln, "Autobiography Written for John L. Scripps, circa June, 1860," *The Collected Works of Abraham Lincoln*, ed. Roy P. Basler (New Brunswick, NJ: Rutgers University Press, 1953), 4:62.

13. Proclus, *A Commentary on the First Book of Euclid's Elements, Translated with Introduction and Notes by Glenn R. Morrow* (Princeton, NJ: Princeton University Press, 1970), 159.

14. David Hirsch and Dan Van Haften, *Abraham Lincoln and the Structure of Reason* (El Dorado Hills, CA: Savas Beatie, 2010).

15. Abraham Lincoln, "Mr. Lincoln's Rejoinder, Fourth Debate with Stephen A. Douglas at Charleston, Illinois, September 18, 1858," *The Collected Works of Abraham Lincoln,* ed. Roy P. Basler (New Brunswick, NJ: Rutgers University Press, 1953), 3:186.

16. Abraham Lincoln, "Speech at Columbus, Ohio, September 16, 1859," *The Collected Works of Abraham Lincoln*, ed. Roy P. Basler (New Brunswick, NJ: Rutgers University Press, 1953), 3:416-417.

17. Milton H. Shutes, *Lincoln and California* (Stanford University, CA: Stanford University Press, 1943), 250. We were unable to independently confirm that the quoted conversation actually occurred. But even if it did not, it somewhat accurately describes the effect of the six elements.

18. The Thomas Jefferson Papers, "Thomas Jefferson to Edward Everett, April 8, 1826," The Library of Congress, www.loc.gov/resource/mtj1.055_0985_0986 (accessed May 6, 2016).

19. Milton H. Shutes, *Lincoln and California* (Stanford University, CA: Stanford University Press, 1943), 250.

20. See David Hirsch and Dan Van Haften, "The Structure of Reason," www.thestructureof reason.com/declaration-of-independence (accessed May 6, 2016).

21. David Hirsch and Dan Van Haften, *Barack Obama, Abraham Lincoln and the Structure of Reason* (El Dorado Hills, CA: Savas Beatie, 2012).

22. David Hirsch and Dan Van Haften, *Barack Obama, Abraham Lincoln and the Structure of Reason* (El Dorado Hills, CA: Savas Beatie, 2012), 9-17; Barack Obama, "Remarks by the President at a Memorial Service for the Victims of the Shooting in Tucson, Arizona," The White House Office of the Press Secretary, www.whitehouse.gov/the-press-office/2011/01/12/remarks-president-barack-obama-memorial-service-victims-shooting-tucson (accessed May 6, 2016). See the video at Barack Obama, "President Obama: Memorial in Arizona," The White House Office of the Press Secretary, www.whitehouse.gov/photos-and-video/video/2011/01/12/president-obama-memorial-arizona (accessed May 6, 2016).

23. Gustav Niebuhr, "Obama's 'Gettysburg Moment': For Us, the Living," *The Huffington Post*, www.huffingtonpost.com/gustav-niebuhr/obamas-gettysburg-moment-_b_808524 .html (accessed May 6, 2016).

24. John McCain, "After the Shootings, Obama Reminds the Nation of the Golden Rule," *The Washington Post*, www.washingtonpost.com/wp-dyn/content/article/2011/01/14/AR201 1011403871.html (accessed May 6, 2016).

25. Peggy Noonan, "Obama Rises to the Challenge," *Wall Street Journal*, online.wsj.com/ article/SB10001424052748703583404576080303941795040.html (accessed May 6, 2016).

26. Russell Allyn, "Obama's Tucson Speech was his Gettysburg Address," *LA Progressive Examiner*, www.examiner.com/progressive-in-los-angeles/obama-s-tucson-speech-was-his-gettysburg-address (accessed May 6, 2016).

27. David Hirsch and Dan Van Haften, "The Structure of Reason," www.thestructureof reason.com/barack-obama-abraham-lincoln-and-the-structure-of-reason/colbert-nails-it (accessed March 17, 2016).

28. David Hirsch and Dan Van Haften, "The Structure of Reason," www.thestructureof reason.com/barack-obama-abraham-lincoln-and-the-structure-of-reason/arithmetic--bill-clinton (accessed March 17, 2016).

29. David Hirsch and Dan Van Haften, "The Structure of Reason," www.thestructureof reason.com/barack-obama-abraham-lincoln-and-the-structure-of-reason/first-lady (accessed March 17, 2016).

Index

The Authors

David Hirsch is an attorney in Des Moines, Iowa. He has a BS from Michigan State University and a JD, with distinction, from the University of Iowa College of Law. He clerked for an Iowa Supreme Court Justice from 1973-1974. In addition to a diversified "small town" law practice, Hirsch was a columnist for the *American Bar Association Journal* for over a decade. Hirsch is admitted to practice in all Iowa state trial and appellate courts, plus: United States Supreme Court, United States Court of Appeals for the Eighth Circuit, United States District Court for the Southern District of Iowa, United States District Court for the Northern District of Iowa, United States Court of Claims, United States Tax Court

Dan Van Haften lives in Batavia, Illinois. He has BS, with high honor, and MS degrees in mathematics from Michigan State University, and a Ph.D. in electrical engineering from Stevens Institute of Technology. He began his career with AT&T Bell Laboratories in 1970, and retired from Alcatel-Lucent in 2007. He worked on telecommunication software development and system testing. He presently writes full time.

Visit their website at www.thestructureofreason.com.

Also by David Hirsch and Dan Van Haften

Abraham Lincoln and the Structure of Reason

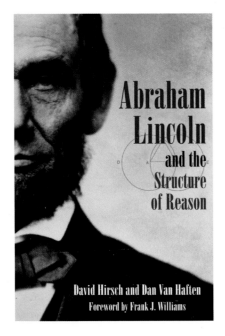

With one year of formal education, and a lifetime of self-study, Abraham Lincoln applied the scientific method to structure iron logic. That method resulted in compelling reason, convincing oratory, and memorable writing. Authors Hirsch and Van Haften persuasively argue, for the first time, that it was Lincoln's in-depth study of geometry that gave the sixteenth President of the United States his verbal structure. Lincoln's fascination with geometry is well documented. But Hirsch and Van Haften were the first to dig beneath the surface. *Abraham Lincoln and the Structure of Reason* demonstrates Lincoln's use of the six elements of a proposition in Lincoln's Cooper Union speech, his First and Second Inaugurals, his legal practice, and in much of his substantive communication from 1854 on.

"A brilliant study...The authors conclusively demonstrate how the self-taught Lincoln mastered Euclidean Geometry and used Euclid's elements in his most famous speeches...To David Hirsch and Dan Van Haften, all students of Abraham Lincoln and our democracy are indebted."
— **Frank J. Williams**, Chair, The Lincoln Forum, and Retired Chief Justice of the Rhode Island Supreme Court

"...one of the most stunningly original works on Abraham Lincoln to appear in years...Hirsch and Van Haften show us how Lincoln applied the Euclidean logic of geometry to the language of law and politics."
— **John Stauffer**, Harvard University English and History Professor